The Dewsburys

For Elaine

Acknowledgements to Private Eye
Thanks to Vic

Published by Prion Books
An imprint of the Carlton Publishing Group
20 Mortimer Street, London W1T 3JW
Text and Pictures Copyright © 2006 Banx
Design Copyright © 2006 Carlton Books Ltd

ISBN-13: 978-1-85375-610-8
ISBN-10: 1-85375-610-5

Printed in Singapore

10 9 8 7 6 5 4 3 2 1

The Dewsburys

SCENES FROM A SUBURBAN MARRIAGE

BY BANX

PRION

BANX HAS BEEN A PROFESSIONAL CARTOONIST FOR THE LAST 25 YEARS. HIS CARTOONS AND STRIPS HAVE APPEARED IN MANY MAGAZINES, BOOKS AND NEWSPAPERS ALL OVER THE WORLD.

HE HAS BEEN PUBLISHED IN *PUNCH*, *PRIVATE EYE*, *SHE*, *THE MAIL ON SUNDAY*, *THE NEW STATESMAN* AND *THE DAILY EXPRESS*. HE HAS BEEN THE *FINANCIAL TIMES*' DAILY CARTOONIST SINCE 1989.

His cartoon animation series **THE MANY DEATHS OF NORMAN SPITTAL**, (MADE WITH BOB GODFREY FILMS) HAS BEEN SHOWN REGULARLY ON TELEVISION. HE LIVES IN GREENWICH, LONDON, AND MAINTAINS A WEBSITE AT **WWW.BANXCARTOONS.CO.UK**

"HE'S NEVER ACTUALLY CAUGHT A SPIDER."

"YOU SPEND TOO LONG ON THE TOILET."

"I NOTICE HE'S *MY* TORTOISE WHEN HE MISBEHAVES."

"WHEN EVERYONE WORE HATS, HE WORE HIS AT AN UNUSUALLY RAKISH ANGLE."

"HE OFTEN PULLS A SICKIE WHEN THE WEATHER'S NICE."

"It started out as *my* pedestal."

"I THOUGHT I SAW A CURTAIN TWITCHING."

"PENNY FOR YOUR THOUGHTS?"

"HE'S RATHER GOOD AT RETRIEVING MY THONG."

"WE'VE NEVER FAKED AN ORGASM TOGETHER BEFORE."

"It's not yoga – he's biting his toenails."

"I THOUGHT VIDEOING OURSELVES IN BED WOULD BE MORE FUN THAN THIS."

"THERE YOU GO — LISTENING DOWN TO ME AGAIN."

"THE SUSPENSE IS KILLING ME – ARE YOU OR AREN'T YOU GOING TO FART?"

"HE WAS ANNOYING ME SO I SET THE CAT ON HIM."

"Do you have to jangle your change every time you cross your legs?"

"Ignore him — he's lonely."

WATER BED

"THE NEIGHBOURS ARE HAVING A LOT OF FOREPLAY TONIGHT."

"NOTICE HOW THE EYES FOLLOW YOU ROUND THE ROOM."

"Does my bum look big in this?"

"HIS HAIR TRANSPLANT REJECTED HIM."

"THAT'S A TYPICAL WOMAN'S GENERALISATION."

"I MISSED THE BOWL AGAIN."

"I asked him to find my clitoris."

"DO YOU HAVE TO MAKE SO MUCH NOISE WHEN YOU COME?"

"Don't lie to me – you've been to the pub again."

"I'VE ASKED YOU NOT TO WEE IN THE FOOTSPA."

"YOU'D BETTER REALLY BE ILL."

"STOP MOANING – IT'S MY TURN ON TOP."

"You never listen to a word I think."

"I DREAD GLOBAL WARMING."

"HE'S TENDED IT FROM SEED."

"At least my stalker didn't forget Valentine's Day."

"HE ALWAYS RUINS THE POCKETS OF HIS TROUSERS."

"HAVE YOU BEEN TALKING TO THE PLANT AGAIN?"

"ALRIGHT, ALRIGHT — I'LL BITE YOUR TOENAILS, BUT
I'M NOT PREPARED TO SWALLOW."

"My wife thinks I'm in the toilet."

"YOU DON'T GO 'VROOM, VROOM' ANYMORE."

"I miss the Christmas decorations."

"Why don't you admit it? We're lost."

"NOT MUCH OF A WIFE-SWAPPING PARTY THOUGH, IS IT?"